*On the
Philadelphian Gold*

By
Philochrysus & Philadelphus

Copyright © 2021 Lamp of Trismegistus. All rights reserved. No part of this publication may be reproduced or transmitted in any form or by any means, electronic or mechanical, including photocopying, recording, or by any information storage and retrieval system, without permission in writing from Lamp of Trismegistus. Reviewers may quote brief passages.

ISBN: 978-1-63118-511-3

Esoteric Classics:
Studies in Alchemy

Other Books in this Series and Related Titles

Aurora of the Philosophers by Paracelsus (978-1-63118-507-6)

The Stone of the Philosophers by A E Waite (978-1-63118-509-0)

The Magician's Heavenly Chaos by Thomas Vaughan (978-1-63118-500-7)

Paracelsus, the Four Elements and Their Spirits by M P Hall (978-1-63118-400-0)

Alchemy in the Nineteenth Century by Helena P. Blavatsky (978-1-63118-446-8)

Cloud Upon the Sanctuary by Waite & K Eckartshausen (978-1-63118-438-3)

The Rosicrucian Chemical Marriage by Christian Rosenkreuz (978-1-63118-458-1)

The Golden Verses of Pythagoras: Five Translations (978-1-63118-479-6)

The Hymns of Hermes by G. R. S. Mead (978-1-63118-405-5)

The Devil in Love by Jacques Cazotte (978–1–63118–499–4)

On the Cave of the Nymphs in the Odyssey by Thomas Taylor (978-1-63118-505-2)

Plato and Platonism and Related Esoteric Essays by various (978-1-63118-432-1)

Clairvoyance and Psychic Abilities by A Besant &c (978-1-63118-403-1)

The Book of Wisdom of Solomon by King Solomon (978-1-63118-502-1)

A Collection of Early Writings on Astral Travel (978-1-63118-477-2)

Rosicrucian Rules, Secret Signs, Codes and Symbols by various (978-1-63118-488-8)

The Sepher Yetzirah and the Qabalah by M P Hall (978-1-63118-481-9)

Arcane Formulas or Mental Alchemy by W W Atkinson (978-1-63118-459-8)

The Machinery of the Mind by Dion Fortune (978-1-63118-451-2)

Brothers & Builders by Joseph Fort Newton (978-1-63118-506-9)

The Leadbeater Reader: A Selection of Occult Essays (978-1-63118-483-3)

Audio versions are also available on Audible, Amazon and Apple

Other Books in this Series and Related Titles

Atlantis, the Gods of Antiquity and the Myth of the Dying God (978–1–63118–498–7)

The Mysteries of Freemasonry & the Druids by M P Hall &c (978-1-63118-444-4)

Prashna Upanishad and Commentary by Charles Johnston (978-1-63118-494-9)

The Kabbalah of Masonry & Related Writings by E Levi &c (978-1-63118-453-6)

The Legend of the Holy Grail and its Connection with Templars and Freemasons by A E Waite (978-1-63118-462-8)

The First and Second Gospels of the Infancy of Jesus Christ by Thomas and James (978-1-63118-415-4)

The Secrets of Enoch by Enoch (978-1-63118-449-9)

Brothers & Builders by Joseph Fort Newton (978-1-63118-506-9)

Magical Essays and Instructions by Florence Farr (978-1-63118-418-5)

Masonic and Rosicrucian History by M P Hall & H Voorhis (978-1-63118-486-4)

History and Teachings of the Rosicrucians by W W Westcott &c (978-1-63118-487-1)

The Smoky God or A Voyage to the Inner World by Emerson (978-1-63118-423-9)

The Janeites, The Man Who Would Be King and Other Stories of Freemasonry by Rudyard Kipling (978–1–63118–480–2)

Gnosis of the Mind by G. R. S. Mead (978-1-63118-408-6)

The Master Mason's Handbook by J S M Ward (978-1-63118-474-1)

The Feminine Occult by various authors (978-1-63118-711-7)

The Leadbeater Reader: A Selection of Occult Essays (978-1-63118-483-3)

The Human Aura: Astral Colors and Thought Forms (978-1-63118-419-2)

The Path of Light: A Manual of Maha-Yana Buddhism (978-1-63118-471-0)

The Hymn of Jesus by G. R. S. Mead (978-1-63118-492-5)

Audio versions are also available on Audible, Amazon and Apple

Table of Contents

Introduction

Page 7

*A Conference Betwixt
Philochrysus & Philadelphus
On the Philadelphian Gold*

Page 9

INTRODUCTION

The word "esoteric" can be difficult to define. Esotericism in general can be seen less as a system of beliefs and more as a category, which encompasses numerous, different systems of beliefs. It's a bit of juxtaposition, since the word "esoteric" indicates something that few people know about, while the term itself broadly covers numerous philosophies, practices, areas of study and belief systems.

In a greater sense, Esotericism acts as a storehouse for secret knowledge, which is often considered ancient (*by tradition, if not by fact*), passed down from generation to generation, in private. At various times in history, simply possessing the knowledge of some of these subjects, was considered illegal and a jailable offence, if discovered. This usually included such general topics as Alchemy, Pharmacology, Qabalah, Hermeticism, Occultism, Ceremonial Magic, Astrology, Divination, Rosicrucianism and so on. Collectively, these areas of study were often referred to as the esoteric sciences.

Sometimes, the outer garment of a subject isn't esoteric, while what is hidden beneath it, is. As an example, Freemasonry isn't necessarily esoteric by nature (at *least not anymore*), but certain signs, passwords and handshakes given to the candidate during their initiation, are in fact, esoteric, in the sense that they are hidden from the general public.

Today, in the twenty-first century, such topics are readily available at bookstores across the country, and numerous mainsteam publishers offer beginners guides and coffee-table volumes on many of these subjects, intended for mass appeal. Books like "*The Secret*" have turned previously arcane topics into household knowledge. All that being the case, however, it isn't to say that there still aren't buried secrets to uncover, ancient wisdom being ignored and forgotten mysteries to be explored. In fact, it is often that we are only able to further our own studies by standing on the shoulders of these disappearing giants.

Lamp of Trismegistus is doing its part to help preserve humanity's esoteric history by making some of these classics available to those students who are seeking to unearth the knowledge of these ancient colossi.

So, be sure to check other titles from our *Esoteric Classics* series, as well as our *Occult Fiction*, *Theosophical Classics*, *Foundations of Freemasonry Series*, *Supernatural Fiction*, *Paranormal Research Series*, *Studies in Buddhism* and our *Christian Apocrypha Series*. You can also download the audio versions of most of these titles from Amazon, Apple or Audible, for learning on the go.

A CONFERENCE BETWIXT
Philochrysus & Philadelphus
ON THE PHILADELPHIAN GOLD

Philochrysus: This was upon me to ask you. You may remember then that you told me how the description of your city which we then read, was more literal, than is easy to be believed, and withal more mystical than it is possible for the wisest of mortals to comprehend. And in particular you told me that it was built first of true and substantial Gold; secondly of fine Gold; thirdly of transparent or glassy Gold; and fourthly of living Gold.

I desire now that you would answer me to all these particulars in order. Do you then say that this city is built of true Gold, and that it is not only metaphorically said to be built of Gold? Is it as real and substantial, is it as visible and palpable, and has it as many good qualities as this which I have now in my hand?

Philadelphus: Yes, Philochrysus, I can assure you that it is built of true and not metaphorical Gold, as some would have it only to be. This Gold, I say, is no less real and substantial, and no less visible and palpable to its inhabitants and has as many, yea more, good qualities that that which you hold in your hand, and seem so pleased with. I know that this is a strange language, and I shall have much ado to make myself understood by you but in any degree. Because I must speak of that which you have never seen, or handled; though others have both seen and handled of it, and you also may come in time to do the same. So that it will be almost as hard a matter for one that is born blind to understand the philosophy of colours, or one born deaf the nature and distinction of sounds, as for you to comprehend what I am about to say of a certain substance that is visible to some but not to you, palpable to some but not to you; and which therefore you have no kind of apprehension of.

Philochrysus: I promise to be very attentive. Do me the favour but to satisfy me as far as you can.

Philadelphus: Well, I will endeavour your satisfaction, after that you shall have answered me a question or two that I have to propose to you.

Philochrysus: I am very ready to do it.

Philadelphus: Why do ye believe that piece of Gold which ye showed me, to be true, real and substantial, and not shadowy, figurative and accidental?

Philochrysus: Why do I believe so? I am not such a stranger to the truth, as not to be able to distinguish it from a shadow. A shadow will fly from me if I go to catch at it, but this I can grasp fast enough. A shadow depends on the substance, and on the position of the Sun which casts it. It has no figure but from the substance, and that is always very faint and weak; it cannot be touched, it has no ponderosity, no light, no power in it. But this is ponderous, bright and powerful. You see me touch it, and its figure is not faint or weak but vivid and strong, without depending upon anything else. Wherever I move it, and whatever the position of it may be to the Sun or light, it still retains the same shape and the same substance. And now I have it fast, I dare venture its flying away.

Philadelphus: I see you are well satisfied with yourself. But pray tell me, how would you give a description of it, to satisfy another that had never seen it, or perhaps never heard of it; or if ever heard of it, yet not otherwise than as a figurative sound to please children with, or as a rattle, a picture, a shadow, a name without substance, without reality? How would you make it to be understood to a Philosopher, and how to a merchant that is no philosopher, supposing them both to be strangers to the nature and use of this sovereign metal?

Philochrysus: Truly, Philadelphus, you begin to puzzle me. And besides I cannot see whither all your windings and turnings will at last lead me. Indeed, it would be a difficult matter to resolve satisfactorily either a Philosopher or a merchant concerning this dear precious metal, if they have not some manner of notice of it beforehand. But since it is not unlawful to make such a supposition, I am ready also to make such an answer as I can.

I would therefore endeavour to satisfy them, by making use of such ideas, images and conceptions which they are already acquainted with; and by compounding them and dividing them, I would strive to frame in the inquirer an idea, image and conception hereof, which might approach as near as possible to the truth. As for instance, if I were to discourse with a philosopher, whom I will suppose, to live in the remotest part of Tartary, or in some dark corner near to the Northern Pole where mines of Gold were never so much as heard of, and no name even found for it in the language of the country. I would think in the first place what to call it, that he might in some sort apprehend me, while I am discoursing with him. Now because some Copper mines may be near to him, and he may have both seen and handled and also tried several experiments upon this metal, therefore I will call it fine Copper or perhaps fine Brass, if this be likewise known to him. Then because I must speak to him in his own terms, and he has used himself to those of Mercury and Sulphur, I will tell him this fine Copper is compounded of a pure Mercurial Water and a pure Sulphureous earth, exactly proportioned and duly maturated and concocted by the Sun-beams in some proper matrix or vessel.

Next I will, as far as I am able, show him the difference, both in quantity and quality, of the compounding principles of this fine Copper, and of his Copper. Whereupon I tell him that the Mercurial Water, which enters into the composition of this fine Copper, is not only more subtle, defecated and pure, than that which is in that Gothic Copper of his, but also that it is there in a much greater quantity. Likewise I tell him that the quantity of the Brimstone or Sulphureous Earth, which enters into the composition of the Gothic copper is greater than that which is in this fine (which I call for distinction the Peruvian) Copper, but that in the former it is more coarse than in the latter. Herein lies the main difference of the Peruvian and the Gothic Copper (which I must make my philosopher understand) as to the composition of the principles both in the one and the other. Which are both essentially the same, but diversified as well according to quality as quantity. He must then confess to me, that the Mercury in the Gothic Copper must needs be originally infected and poisoned, and that there must be a defect in its proportion: as likewise that the coarseness, the superfluity and the combustibleness of its Sulphur are no inconsiderable impediments to the perfection of this metal. And he will grant me to this, I believe, though he never have seen the fine metal of Peru, that there may be such a Copper there found as I do describe, if there may be but a Mercury, or water of Life, freed from its original infection and poison, and then fitly adapted and conjoined with a proper Sulphur that shall be pure and of an incombustible nature, so as not to diminish in the severest fires.

However perhaps he will maintain, that I ought not altogether to despise the Sulphureous Earth of his Gothick Copper; for that though it were not so pure, fixed and permanent as that of the other, yet it was of the very same essence and nature with it, and therefore also might possibly come to be in like manner purified and made incombustible.

And when I have brought him thus far, then I may speak unto him of the several properties of our fine copper, and leave him to compare them with those of that coarse sort which is only known to him. And here if I could give him an exact calculation of the weight of a cubical inch of the Peruvian

Copper, comparing it with a cubical inch of the Gothick and showing the preponderancy of that above this, I should settle in him a just idea as to one property of it. Another property is purity and clarity, which I must in the next place give him to understand by deduction from such ideas or conceptions which he has already admitted. A third is its tincture, and here as I must heighten that idea which he has entertained on one side, so I must lessen it on the other, that this man may exactly quadrate with the original. A fourth and main property which I am to tell him of is Fixation, or the immortality and indefectibility of the tincture, life or soul of this metallic body. Besides all which I may in the fifth place discourse to him of the extreme ductability or rarefaction of it; if it might not be too prodigious for his belief; and sixthly, of its medicinal uses and qualities, which would afford me a great variety of matters to entertain him with.

And thus I shall have in some degree satisfied my Tartarian or my Gothick Philosopher, that the fine Copper of Peru is not metaphorical or symbolical, as his poor country men, who have never seen it, would persuade him: but that it is as truly, really and substantially of a metallic nature and consistence, as that which he daily handles for such. And he now begins to understand how this fine copper, which I otherwise call Gold, is compounded of the same (yet better graduated) principles, with a more exact proportion than his, and that it is not metaphorically, but really a metallic substance, more ponderous, and brighter than the other, also of a bitter (though not so deep) Tincture, more fixed and ductile, and lastly more proper for human bodies, to be used internally or externally, when prepared according to Art.

So I take my leave of my Philosopher, and go next to my merchant. Here I shall not have so much to do, as with the former. I need only to mind him in brief of the several properties about which I discoursed my philosopher, and then declare unto him the great and excellent use thereof in commerce, so as more than four hundred times to answer the other in common valuation, and often more than five hundred.

Philadelphus: Tis enough, I find you like well the subject that you are upon, but hope it will serve to lead you into one that is far better. Of all that you have now said, nothing will be found to be in vain, when I shall come to examine you. The tables may come perhaps to be turned upon yourself. Wherefore let me persuade you to try thoroughly, whether that be indeed gold, which you believe to be so. But since you have been pleased to satisfy me as to what I demanded, I am now most ready to satisfy you, as to what was propounded; only I must first premise two or three things that I may be understood by you. Wherefore be now attentive and consider well what I am about to say.

Philochrysus: I will be sure Sir, to attend your motion, for I begin to be very jealous, that you have been carrying on all this while some plot to undermine me. But pray let us hear your premises, and I promise to make the best use of all the ears and eyes which I have.

Philadelphus: The first thing that I wish then to premise is this, That the Divine Blessing was originally spoken forth upon the whole Creation of God. Or as some would rather choose to express it - It was outspoken into the Creation, that is, by a real, vital and essential infusion engrafted into it. So that whatever come out of the hands of God was good. No evil should ever be derived from the Divine Being, who notwithstanding the supreme liberty of Will, is necessitated when He acts, to act according to Goodness. No sin nor death, no barrenness or drought, no weakness or disproportion could at all proceed from him. Wherefore he rejoicing, as it were, in the works of his hands, pronounced them both severally and universally to be good, yea very good, as considered in their whole system, and harmonious union with each other.

Philochrysus: I must grant that you say. But I would fain see to what purpose It will serve you.

Philadelphus: You may yet, before we part.

Philochrysus: I cannot deny but that God blessed the whole Creation and that all the works of his hands are good. Make your best of it.

Philadelphus: The second thing that I have to premise is but as a corollary from the former, and is strengthened by universal experience. It is this, The Works of the Creation are not Now in the same State, as they were when they first came out of the hands of God, or as when the Divine Blessing was pronounced upon them, or outspoken onto them, yet with this limitation, so far as they are within our Sphere or Orb. For experience doth at this day too sufficiently attest that the creatures, whether they be of the animal, vegetable or mineral kingdom, cannot be all said to be good, howsoever they be considered, either separately by themselves, or conjunctly in harmony with the rest. And whatever may be pleaded on their behalf by some acute philosophers and divines, that all the creatures are, even at this day, good; though not positively, yet relatively, and with respect both to their present constitution and the constitution of the world in general, it is evident, to me at least, if either the undoubted records of scripture, or the natural light of reason may judge of the appeal, that all that they can say will, if it prove anything, certainly conduce to the very overturning of the positive goodness of the Divine Being, and the introducing in the room thereof a certain relative, hypothetical and imaginary goodness, and to the building up a very odd and irregular system of the Universe.

This if it were necessary, I might at large deduce through several particulars, proving the absurdity and inconsistency of such a supposition, that has been taken up of late by some men of name, and by them too much authorised to the dishonour of God, though they might not perhaps design it so, as I am apt both to hope and believe. But this would lead me out very far and keep me too long from the resolution of the question in hand. However, Philochrysus, if at any other time you think it worth your while to demand a particular satisfaction as to this point, I shall be most willing to give it to you.

Philochrysus: I thank you, Philadelphus. At present I am well enough satisfied in this matter; yea so much as I have often with myself admired, even when bit by a flea, how any could be serious in pleading for the perfection of the present constitution of the World of Nature, as if it never had been better, or was never to be better; but after it shall have lasted out such a term, that it must return back again into its primitive state of nothingness; by the most dreadful dissolution through Fire. This their catastrophe of Our World, I must confess, did never very well please me; but did always stick.

Philadelphus: It is then granted by you that the present constitution of this terrestrial world in which we live, is not so perfect and good as it was originally brought forth by God, and that it may, by the gift of god, recover again its original constitution.

Philochrysus: It is granted.

Philadelphus: Well! Answer me now this one question. Which do you now think best deserves to be called by this or that name, that which is most perfect in its kind, and that which comes up most really to the true and original frame of its nature, or that which falls short of it, and is very Imperfect as to its kind?

As for instance, you take two sheep, or two horses, and of these let one be placed at the right hand and the other at the left. Suppose now the horse at the right hand to have all the most excellent features and proportions of an horse, and that at the left to have none of them at all, but to be very mean and despicable. Suppose also the sheep at the right hand, to be very plump and fat, and to wear a Golden Fleece upon its back, and that at the left to be lean, deformed and leprous. Will you hereupon say that the horse at the left hand is a real horse, but that at the right a metaphorical one? Or that the sheep at the left is a true sheep, but not that at the right? And will you not rather say that these by approaching nearer to the perfection of their nature, and to the original integrity and beauty in which they were first both brought forth from the Divine exemplar, do less deserve to be called figurative or allegorical than the other.

Philochrysus: So indeed it seems to me, if either of these may be called a figurative sheep, or a figurative horse, it must be the left-handed ones, who come not up to the primitive constitution of their nature, into which the divine blessing was spoken, but have fallen under the curse, and suffered the depravation of their first pure form, according to the supposition that is granted you. And if any one had ever seen such and other but such lean and deformed sheep, or such ill conditioned and disproportioned jakes, verily I say should much condemn his rashness, if he should say there were no other, but positively conclude these to be the best of the kind, and that above them are but hypothetical metaphors, or poetical expressions of somewhat transcending nature. Yea I should be a little angry if he should be so obstinate as to stand out against the authentic relations of ocular witness, or go to oblige me to deny my own senses, because his have not had the same experience which mine also had.

Philadelphus: Suppose also that you have two bushels of wheat, the one whereof is half full of chaff, the other perfectly cleansed, the one blighted, the other large grained and sound. Would you say that the blighted and chaffy corn is only real and substantial, but the sound and the cleansed to be no more than a metaphor or a shadow. I believe not.

Suppose once more that you have two pips of Spanish wine, the one natural and unsophisticated, clean and sprightly, the other pipe sophisticated and filled up half with water: and that you have tasted only of the latter. Would you say that this only is true wine, and not the other?

Philochrysus: No, Philadelphus, I think I should not so far expose my own judgment. And though I should not have tasted of the finest wine, yet would I not say there is no better than that I have tasted; and assert that what I am told of the other is only fancy or figure.

Philadelphus: Now my dear Philochrysus, Hold to your words. For I see two pieces of gold, the one as at your right hand, the other is at your left, the one celestial gold, the other terrestrial gold, like as there are bodies celestial and bodied terrestrial. The gold of your left hand you see and handle, and say therefore that it is substantial. The gold of the right hand you see not neither can you handle, and conclude therefore that it is shadowy. The reason whereof is this. The former has a peculiar virtue in it to blind that eye by which the former Gold may be discerned, and to induce such a paralytic numbness and deadness on all one part of the man that has a lust after it, that he cannot possibly feel or handle the other till his disease be first removed from him. But as for me, that Gold which you call substantial, I should of the two rather choose to call shadowy Gold, and that which you think to be shadowy and figurative, I must call substantial and real, on far greater reasons than you have produced to move me to the contrary.

Philochrysus: I cannot but believe my senses. You shall not easily persuade me out of them. For if they deceive me, I can be certain of nothing.

Philadelphus: Be not afraid: you may keep your senses still for me. Since the senses deceive none; but it is the judgment which is made upon them that may be erroneous. Take care therefore that you judge not amiss, and think that to be in the object itself which is nothing but an impression produced by it upon the sensory. But tell me, do you ever dream?

Philochrysus: Yes I do.

Philadelphus: You may then remember how you thought that you have seen, felt and handled various objects which have vanished away as soon as you awakened.

Philochrysus: I do. And particularly I call to mind, how I have sometime thought myself to be rolling among bags of gold. So that it has been no small trouble to me to find myself undeceived in the morning.

Philadelphus: Forget not this. The application will not be difficult, and very nearly concerns you, my friend. Philochrysus, you are in a dream at this very instant, and you will certainly find yourself undeceived in the morning, when your senses that are now locked up in sleep shall recover themselves.

Philochrysus: In a dream say you? Nay, then the whole world is a dream. All that I do is dream and fancy, and whatever I behold or handle is but a shadow. Will you make all the world beside yourself to be in a dream? Will you make all the hurly-burlies in it, all the traffickings, negotiations, and wars, with all manner of transactions, private and public, civil and religious, to be nothing more but the sportive imaginations of the night? Will you make nothing to be real or substantial of what is seen, felt, heard or understood by us poor mortals? Sure, Philadelphus, you are no sceptic.

Philadelphus: No, I am an eclectic. But yet I have found the good of scepticism, as to many things that you believe. And if it go not too far, it is the foundation of all solid knowledge, natural, political or divine. Wherefore, however strange it may appear to you, it is not very far from the truth, to say that this world, with all that is in it, is but a dream or a shadow when compared with the invisible worlds. I am afraid to press you too much with these matters, and therefore I only said it is not very far from the truth to say so, but the indubitable records wherein in manifestly the finger of God, would bear me out, if I should say that it is the very truth itself. Search into these and you will find enough to open your eyes and let you see that the form of this World passeth away, and that all that belongs to it is no more than as a vision of the might, which flies away with the day break. My thoughts have been formerly the same with yours: the poisoned cup from the hand of the Fair Harlot, whom I have mentioned to you, cast me into a deep sleep. And in it I remember, I had just the same dreams which you have now. I thought terrestrial gold was as substantial as you imagine it to be, and of the celestial gold I had no manner of apprehension; but was contented to look on it as a figure and not as a substance. But I was roused out of my sleep by a swift messenger out of the Heavenly Philadelphia, upon which all the enchanted scenes of the night immediately fled away, and I awakened recovering the senses which had been before chained up, and then I quickly perceived my errors. Ah! Philochrysus! Awake! Awake! There stands now at your right hand one of the citizens of that beautiful city, who holds before him a medal made of the same gold, which he would present to you, if you would but suffer your eyes to be opened, and would not hold so fast the shadow.

Philochrysus: What mean you to do with me? Oh! A little more sleep, a little more slumber, a little more of this worlds, and then I awake. Disturb me not.

Philadelphus: He talks in his sleep. Ho! Ho! Philochrysus. You will not yet be awakened I find. I will therefore for a little time grant you your heart's desire, and this once, suppose that you are not asleep while you sleep, but that your dream is a reality, and all the conclusions that you have made from the exercise of your outward senses to be true. For by parity of reason (even granting what you say) as you do conclude the terrestrial gold to be true, real and substantial, I do conclude the celestial to be so, and much more so. If you plead sensation for yours, I know those that plead it for ours, and that deserve as much (at least) to be believed as any that you bring. But lest you might not so readily believe or apprehend perhaps the witnesses that I could produce, I will proceed with you as you would do with your Goth or Tartar, that had never heard of the gold mines of Peru. Wherefore I must needs tell you that if the Peruvian gold be true gold, then the Philadelphian gold deserves also of right so to be called, yea is much better qualified of the two to bear this name, as it is more perfect in its kind, and as it more nearly approaches then the former to the true and original frame of pure and undefiled nature, exactly compounded according to the divine exemplar, and duly concocted in the bowels of the everlasting mountains, the mountains of the Sun and the Mountains of the Moon. Whence, supposing the difference of Philadelphian and Peruvian Gold to be, as the difference of Peruvian and Gothic Copper; this will not hinder but that the Philadelphian Gold, both according to the greater purity of its constituent principles (as without the least alloy of the curse) and the most exact proportion of then, may well deserve to be looked on no less real than the Peruvian.

Philochrysus: If it be so, pray dear Philadelphus, give me some of it, that I may make a proof.

Philadelphus: You are not yet out of your dream, you know not what you say. For you neither understand what manner of Gold this is, neither who it is that can give it. It may be called to you by a thousand names, but I do assure you that it is true and proved gold. And let me tell you that your gold, or the false brass of Peru, is not constituted of Principles altogether pure and defected, but mixed with some close and inherent imperfections. Neither are the proportions adjusted according to perfect Nature, but only according to the perfect constitution of this terrestrial orb. The curse that has entered into the whole lower Creation has also entered into this, and it is not a perfect metal, except with respect to the lapsed and broken frame of this our Earth.

Philochrysus: Hah! Philadelphus! I am wondering where you will run at last. I am not so much in a dream, but I can laugh at these amusements of yours. Did ever any before deny Gold to be a perfect metal?

Philadelphus: Mistake me not. I do not deny it to be a perfect metal with respect to the present order of things in their Fallen State. But I do positively aver that it is not a perfect metal with respect to that primitive and original order of Beings which proceeded immediately from God through His Word, wherein and whereby they subsist; but that it partakes of the curse, as well as all the other subjects of the mineral or metallic kingdom, though not in the same degree. Now there is an Inherent curse, and there is also an Adherent Curse, and of both of these it more or less participates.

Philochrysus: Pray what do you mean by an Inherent Curse, and how do you appropriate it to the Terrestrial Gold.

Philadelphus: Know what is the Blessing and you cannot fail to know what is the Curse in Nature. There is an Inherent Blessing in every creature, and there is also an Adherent Blessing. Without the former God could never have pronounced them good, and without the latter they could never have been serviceable to man, or to the rest of their fellow creatures. A privation, or loss, in either of these kinds, is called the Curse. And as it has diverse degrees and is variously specified, so takes it up diverse names, as Death, Darkness, Hades, Sheol, the Turba, the Left Hand, the Seed of the Serpent, the Mist out of the Earth, Lilith, Arimanius, Poison, the Blood of the Old Dragon, the Prisons, the North, and many others.

The benediction now of both kinds may be lessened, hidden or removed either in part of in whole. The Adherent Benediction may possibly admit of a total remove and separation, but the inherent can never do this without the destruction and annihilation of the subject wherein it is. Whence though it may be hid, yet can it never be separated without the entire disunion of its constituent and vital principles. Which are not perishable, but endure the same, notwithstanding all the cortices, veils, and coverings, wherewith they may be overcast or oppressed, and which are said to be under the president-ship of so many evil Angels. Behold then here is Wisdom to take away the Inherent Curse from the creature, and to cause the disappeared Blessing to reappear, and exert forth itself. Now shall you understand how this curse is to be appropriated to the terrestrial Gold, and how the contrary Blessing is to be predicated of the celestial. But in the first place you are to take notice, that as the inherent is here less than in any other subjects of the same Kingdom and Order, so the Adherent Curse is greater. In the second place you are to observe that the primary and Radical principles being (as to us) invisible in themselves, the secondary and elementary, which may be made visible, can be here only examined into. In the third place, I am now to acquaint you that these elementary principles, which I call also Spermatical, as I call the former Seminal, are vastly different in the state of pure and of corrupt Nature.

For in pure nature there is found a bright living crystalline water, full of spirit, power and energy; but in Nature corrupted there is a water that is opposite to this, being without Light, Life, or purity, without spirituality or strength, and void of all benign efficacy. Wherefore as a stagnated pool remote from the sun beams, or as a dead insipid phlegm, is not to be regarded or valued, so likewise there is found a bright, living and crystalline earth (such as hath been, and such as will be, and such as is even at this time, when it appears not, except to some few) which is sometimes compared to fine silver, and is called the Salt of the Earth. And in this Blessed earth is locked up the Spirit, Energy and Seed of the Mineral and vegetable kingdoms in their purest constitution, yea and of the animal too. For that it contains in itself the Fire of Nature, by which the wheel of her Magia, according to all the seven forms and spirits is set to work.

On the contrary there is a dull, dead and opaceous earth that is mixed more or less with all terrestrial subjects, and that may by Art be separated from them. This is the Curse of the Earth which must be taken away and dissolved, before the Blessed and new Earth can appear, wherefore it is called the Damned Earth.

Philochrysus: I hope you will not say that there is any of what the Chymists call Damned Earth in this our Gold. For I cannot bear the thought of it. Pray therefore explain yourself here a little.

Philadelphus: It is you yourself that make the particular application, for I did not. And indeed, Sir, I was almost afraid to touch you so near the quick. But if your Gold, Philochrysus, be a terrestrial subject (which you will scarce deny) then I am sure it must have some share of this Damned earth in it. For the Curse has not a command to stop when it came to a mine of Gold, but like a leaven it passed through and through, and infected the whole earth, and all that belonged to it. There might not indeed so much of it here abide as elsewhere, and therefore I said there was less of the Inherent Curse in this, than in any other subject of the same kingdom or order. Yet there is some, and that too very considerable, if either reason or experience may be allowed to pass the judgment. But this would lead us too far into a Philosophical disquisition.

Let it suffice at present to consider whether what a vulgar and ordinary artist may be able to give an ocular demonstration of in the greatest part of earthly subjects, an expert master may not be as able to give the same in All?

Wherefore be not angry, dear sir, at what I have asserted, but learn to bear the thought of what will be so much your disappointment, as to let you see the fair idol of your heart is not so lovely as you have imagined it to be, and that it is not all true gold that glisters in your hand.

There is a Damned Earth Terra Damnata et Maledicta that cleaves so fast to it, as is not (easily) to be separated by the refiners art. And I am informed from credible testimonies, that whosoever shall be understanding in heart and skillful in hand, to separate this vile earth from the precious Solar Earth in the body of Terrestrial Gold, shall find the quantity of the former (however small when compared to the inferior metals) to exceed the other. And if what is related concerning the degradation of Gold by an eminent and curious eye-witness of this nation, whom all the philosophical and Christian world stands obliged to (and who had this generous and noble design to vindicate Religion from all sectarian polity or partiality, and to establish it upon solid and immutable grounds, be true; and if also the daily experiments) made even in ordinary laboratories of the possibility of its supergradation and Exaltation, by losing in its weight, and so possessing an higher Tincture and Clarity, may deserve any credit: Then is it certain that it may still arrive to an higher degree both of Fixation and Purity, than it could ever meet with in the Bowels of the Accursed earth.

But whether this can ever be quite set free from its Inherent Curse or no, is not so material to our present purpose. However there is a vein, I can assure you, of Paradisical Gold, which not having been with it infected, is by Moses pronounced to be good, (Genesis 2,12). And yet even this is no more to be compared with the Philadelphian or Sionitical Gold, than the Peruvian is with it. Hereby you may, in part I hope apprehend what is meant both by the Blessing and the Curse, which are inherent in this Metallic body.

Philochrysus: I do, I think, pretty well understand you. But pray what do you mean by an Adherent Curse, and how is that to be appropriated to the Terrestrial Gold?

Philadelphus: The Adherent Curse is that which adheres or cleaves to the Creature, by external application, and not by Internal Constitution, or composition. And here by external application I mean not barely any outward abuse of the same whatever, but also (and chiefly) any degree of adhesion of the Human Soul to it, how intrinsic soever, and the more intrinsic still the more dangerous, it being foreign, incongruous, and extrinsic both to the Soul, and to the creature which she seeks to cleave as to her blessing. Now though your terrestrial Gold has indeed not so much of the inherent, yet has it far more of the Adherent Curse, which is much the worst of the two. And though it should be never so perfect as to its composition, that avails not if this other Curse sticks to it. Yea, on the contrary, this will be so much the greater and the heavier, as in the case of the Tartarization (2 Peter, 2,4) of those angels who kept not their first estate of adhesion to the Original Beauty and

Goodness, and in that of the Golden Calf of Israel, concerning which the Jews have to this very day a celebrated proverb, that no punishment is ever inflicted upon them in which there is not some portion of this calf. And I fear the same may be justly applicable not to them alone. What Evil of Sin is there in the whole world that is not perpetrated for the sake of it? And what Evil of pain, or dreadful judgments by the Divine nemesis have not already been pulled down upon particular persons, upon families and upon whole kingdoms? Behold, and consider the times of old; what examples all histories both sacred and profane doth give you. To conclude, how many are there that for the sake of this, labour the greatest part of their lives in the very fire, who at length reap nought but smoke and dross, in the room of those Golden Mountains which they hereby imagined to themselves? And how many weary themselves all their lives for very vanity, while being deceived with the false show of an adhering blessing, they find only misery and repentance; who, had they taken but half that pains to discover the Paradisical or Philadelphian mine of Gold, would never have been left in such plunges at the last? Behold all this proceeds from its Adherent Curse. Remember, prithee Philochrysus, the dying aphorism of the richest Subject of the world at that time, as well as the best politician, and the most faithful servant; which famous aphorism is, I suppose, not unknown to you.

Philochrysus: You mean, I know the saying of that great man, which he left in his legacy to posterity: Had I but taken but half that pains to serve my God, as I took to serve my Prince, he would not now have deserted me.

Philadelphus: I do so. And withal I assure you, my good friend, that if you were but half as diligent in seeking after the celestial, as you are in seeking after the terrestrial Gold, you would be experimentally convinced that I have spoken nothing to you all this while but the very Truth, and you would find yourself possessed of substance instead of vanity.

Philochrysus: I am at a loss. I know not what to make of that which you say. Disturb me not out of my sleep. For I would rather dream on at the old rate, than be molested. Have pity on me, and depart from me. For I am Philochrysus. I am a lover of that what you have contemptibly nick-named terrestrial Gold. The which to me is a Celestial substance. But you will hardly allow it to be a substance at all, that so you may the more exalt the Gold (as you call it) of your own country, which I must call imaginary. Tell me not then that mine is vanity, or the shadow only of a substance. Neither speak to me of labouring for smoke and dross. I know what is substance, I thank my stars, and I can distinguish between what is true and what is counterfeit. Mine hath been tried in the Fire, and weighed in the balance. It hath stood in the one; and in the other hath been found to have its just weight. Can you also pretend to this?

Philadelphus: Yes, more than pretend. Mine is indeed Gold tried in the Fire, and it has been also weighed in the balance as well as yours. And let me tell you besides, that your gold shall never be able to endure this fire-trial, but shall fly away in it as lead and dross. And one grain of the Gold of my

City if put into the balance will preponderate this whole room full of yours. Whence the Crown that is mad out of this Gold is called emphatically a weight of Glory and an Hyperbolical or excessive weight, yea a far exceeding and Hyperbolically Hyperbolical weight (2 Corinthians 4,17). So far exceeds the celestial Gold in preponderosity the terrestrial Gold when weighed together, as no hyperbole can reach. It exceeds in like manner in clarity and lustre, in fixation and permanency, in the superexcellency of its Tincture, in ductibility and divisibility; and in all manner of medicinal uses both for Spirit, Soul and Body, all which it revives, exhilarates and perfects. And in the last place all the merchandise of your World is not to be compared with it. This alone can truly and really and lastingly make you rich. It would not be difficult to particularize each of these, and to show hereby the reality and substantiality of this Gold that I plead for, not only equally with, but far above that which is dug out of the Earth. But all that can be said hereupon, would but serve so much the more to exasperate you if you comprehend it not, or will not attend to it. In vain therefore would it be for me to give you (at present) a particular description of its several properties, as also of its constituent principles and the manner of their union. I must wait to do that till those senses which are fallen asleep in you shall come to be awakened. But I am therefore sent that I might rouse you out of your sleep. Forgive me that I thus wake you. O Philochrysus! what has become of the eye-salve of Sophia? Arise and anoint your eyes.

Philochrysus: Hold! I think I now begin to see. I must confess that I can now see the possibility of what you drive at, but that it is actually so, I cannot yet perceive. I remember I was once a little acquainted with one that might possibly be of your society, and I did hear him exclaim from the pulpit in this manner: "Think ye, ye shall be set up as pillars in the Temple of God to uphold it? or that you shall be full of gold in your pockets, of the finest gold tried in the Fire, like the rich men of the Earth? and to ruffle it in silks, and fine raiment as those in princes' courts? Do you think that these things are here meant in these promises made to the Seven Churches? No, No, dream of no such things, for I say there is not one word true according to the letter.

Philadelphus: I do say that every word, every syllable, every letter is true, and that there are real and substantial pillars in the Temple of God, real and substantial Gold in the City of God, and real and substantial raiment worn by the citizens thereof. And yet at the same time, I do assert that there is no Word, syllable or letter true, if strictly taken according to that low idea which the natural man has fixed to these words. For as much as there is a more than hyperbolical excess in the difference of one from the other. As each property by itself considered will manifest. And if you are convinced of the possibility (at least) of what I have said, you must acknowledge the actual existence hereof. For that there can be no other reason invented whereby you deny it, but its impossibility and inconsistency.

Philochrysus: I resign therefore, and yield to you, that the City of Philadelphia may be built of true, real and substantial Gold, which has nothing of the curse either Inherent or

Adherent sticking to it, according to the sense that the describer means, or that you explain, though not according to that which the natural man would have.

Philadelphus: You comprehend me right. I shall therefore proceed. I said then, in the second place, that it is built of fine Gold, much more fine and higher graduated than any you can ever have seen. This you may in part already understand by what has been said hitherto. But here I shall much more stand in need of words whereby to express myself.

Philochrysus: I long greatly to hear you speak distinctly of this Superfine and supergraduated Gold. I shall not forget what you have said. Therefore proceed on.

Philadelphus: You need but remember your Gothic philosopher. Consider also that there is a twofold body, There is a material and elementary body, and there is an spiritual and a heavenly body. The one is gross, the other fine.

Philochrysus: I can understand perfectly what you mean by the former, but the notion of an immaterial body seems to me the very same contradiction as that of an immaterial substance seemed to an eminent asserter of materialism called Philautus. If you had but him to deal with, he would make work, I believe, with your non-elementary and spiritual body.

Philadelphus: It may be so. But I never feared the strength of reasoning in Philautus, though I know him pretty well, and all his principles whether in Philosophy, Divinity or politics are opposite to mine. He is the express character of the natural man throughout, and in his works everywhere you have the most lively image of the Fallen State of Nature, whereof great advantage may be made by the wise, it being nowhere that I know so deeply and philosophically handled. This indeed he mistakes for the true and original State of Nature; but herein he speaks well enough, and true enough, as a natural or animal Man, and without deviating, most exactly follows his principles wherever they lead him. On the other side the most learned and profound of all his answerers very admirably both describes and demonstrates the true and original state of Nature, such as it was, and such as it shall be again, but not such as it is at present. As for Philautus he is not dead, but lives in his disciples, and will live as long as the present corrupt state of Nature shall remain upon the Earth. For the Psyche in man is never able to penetrate beyond the image; only the pure spirit of Sophia can reach to the life, which is so imaged out in discourse. Hence he who had only the Psyche, was not able to distinguish betwixt the one and the other, but he took them both to be the same. So finding in the origination of several languages that a Spirit was imaged forth or signified by Breath, he presently concludes that the Spirit and Breath were one and the same, and consequently that all Spirits (as such) were material and corporeal beings. he in the like manner, finding in the verbal image of substance was expressed that which stands under, or props up somewhat, entertained immediately a most gross and sensible conception hereof, and tied it down to matter. So then nothing could be a greater absurdity to him, or a more manifest contradiction, than to believe an immaterial substance, that is an immaterial matter. Now among those who have a great and just abhorrence for his sentiments, all are not set free themselves from the very same method of argumentation, as from a numerous induction of instances might be verified if need were.

Wherefore I shall only beg of you what is highly necessary in order to your understanding of what I speak, and to your passing a judgment thereupon, that you content not yourself with the lax and popular sense of a word, as that which is generally very equivocal, but that you seek out the strict and close idea that is to be affixed to it, for the removal of all ambiguity in the terms, and the distinction of the image from its original, or (as the Schools would rather speak) of the Signum from Signatum, the sign from the thing signified.

Philochrysus: It is very just what you require, Phildelphus. None can gainsay this method, after what the celebrated author of An Essay on Human Understanding, together with a French philosopher of the first magnitude , have written on it, shall be looked into. Wherefore tell me in the first place, what you mean by Substance?

Philadelphus: Hereby I understand that which hath both Essence and Existence, being created by God, and made capable of bearing up, or supporting various modes of Being.

Philochrysus: What do you mean by Body?

Philadelphus: Hereby I understand a substance that is extended, and is capable of various modes of Extension. Two of which modes are penetrability and impenetrability.

Philochrysus: Is penetrability then a mode of extension? I always thought that all matter was impenetrable.

Philadelphus: True. All Matter is impenetrable, but all body is not. And penetrability is as much a mode of extension as impenetrability. For where there is no co-extension there is no penetration, and where there is no penetration there can be no life. Without therefore all Nature were dead, it remains that extended substances may be penetrated. Now there are extended substances, or rather one extended substance (of which I may speak to you hereafter) which can penetrate others, but which cannot be penetrated by any. There are also extended substances which can penetrate others by co-extension, and which may themselves also be penetrated by others. lastly there are extended substances or bodies which cannot penetrate others, but which may be penetrated by them. Thus by the outward light of this world, which is a body of the second order, the Earth may be penetrated, which can neither penetrate it or any other substance.

Philochrysus: What do you mean by Matter?

Philadelphus: Hereby I understand a body that is impenetrable, and divisible, and which is capable of various modes of division. So that all Matter is Body, but all Body is not Matter. By impenetrable I mean not that which cannot be at all penetrated, but I mean that which is not to be penetrated by anything of its own order, and which itself can penetrate nothing.

Philochrysus: How can the same Body be impenetrable and divisible?

Philadelphus: Because it is impenetrable, therefore it is divisible into parts. For if it could be penetrated, then would there be no need of division, or separation of the parts? Wherefore that which is penetrable is also indivisible, or rather indiscerpible, and consequently incorruptible.

Philochrysus: I comprehend your meaning. And now I conceive what is your notion of an immaterial or Spiritual Body called likewise a Non-elementary (which is a Quintessential) or heavenly Body; Namely, that it is an extended substance, penetrable, penetrative, indivisible, indiscernible, and incorruptible. As on the contrary your notion of a material and elementary body must be this, that it is an extended substance, impenetrable, penetrated, divisible, discerpible and corruptible. I begin consequently to understand a little your notion of Material and Spiritual, of Elementary and Heavenly Gold, and why you call the one gross and the other fine Gold. But notwithstanding that I conceive how the Material and Elementary Gold is an extended Substance which is impenetrable to all terrestrial bodies, and may be penetrated by the Celestial, which is also divisible into parts, yea Discerpible into the minutest atoms, yet can I not easily yield that it should be corruptible.

Philadelphus: All that is compounded of Elements must be more or less corruptible. And though certain elementary bodies may have arrived at some degree of incorruptibility, yet it is but a degree, it being impossible for them to be ever perfectly freed from corruption, but by a dissolution and a resuscitation. For this is a most assured maxim, that all things must be perfected upon the cross and all things must be tried by Fire Without passing through the Cross there is no resurrection, without passing through the Fire there is no Fixation or Incorruption, no Purification or Spiritualization. Hence the messenger of the Covenant of Immortality is by a certain prophet compared to a refiners Fire, who saith of him that he shall purify the Priesthood and purge them as Gold that they may rightly offer the sacrifice of Minha to Jehovah. Hence also a great and wise King saith, the word (or outflowing emanation of the Lord is refined; and again he cries out Thy Word is exceedingly refined most fine and pure. And likewise this very Word of the Lord or the Word the Lord saith to the shepherds of Israel: I will refine them as Silver is refined, and will try them as Gold is tried. And elsewhere he saith, I have refined thee melted thee down, and then brought thee out of the furnace. For this cause the precious Sons of Zion are compared to fine gold, and the Angelical man who appeared to Daniel had his loins Girded with fine Gold of Ophir. From this also an account may be given why the Altar of Incense was made of refined Gold, together with the Ark and the Cherubims, also why Wisdom's oracle is so often compared to fine Gold; and lastly why the Shulamite describes both the head and the feet of her beloved to be as of fine Gold, that is such an indivisible, indiscerpible and incorruptible substance, as being extended is therefore a body, and as possessing all the properties of the material and gross Gold, is therefore a spiritual body, or immaterial and celestial gold.

Philochrysus: I must confess that I have always taken a spiritual body to be a contradiction in terms, for I never heard otherwise before but that Spirit and Body were contraries. But now I begin to mistrust that I have not been used rightly to apply ideas to words.

Philadelphus: Your diffidence is well grounded. For I do not find that Spirit and Body are anywhere opposed as contraries in those writings which command the greatest authority and deference above all others to them. I find indeed frequently spirit and flesh to be set as opposites, but spirit and body never. Nay I find it there expressly asserted that there is a natural body, and there is a spiritual body. And so in like manner there is a natural Gold and there is a spiritual, which surpasseth the former, as the spiritual Body of the Resurrection doth this Natural and Elementary body which we now wear about us. Moreover the same highly mystic author tells those who being immersed in the flesh had no notion of a Spiritual or Heavenly Body, any more than you had.

There are also Celestial Bodies (of a spiritual and heavenly property) and Bodies Terrestrial (of a material and earthly property as common gold but the Glory of the Celestial is one, and the glory of the Terrestrial is another; that is, the glory of the Philadelphian Gold differs from the glory of the Peruvian, as far as heaven is from Earth.

Philochrysus: You extremely amaze me, good Philadelphus, to tell me that the City from whence you are named is built of such fine gold. But pray now go on, if you are not weary, to satisfy me in the third place, whether it be built of Transparent and Glassy Gold.

Philadelphus: Be not over hasty, but take time to meditate upon what I (through the assistance of the Good Spirit) have freely communicated to you. Neither have I done yet with the former, for I am not yet come to the top of the ladder with you. Perhaps your head may be giddy in endeavouring to reach it at this present. Wherefore though I cannot be ever weary of discoursing these matters, yet I will now take my leave of you with one parallel instance, which you may digest against we meet the next time. Consider what difference there is betwixt the faeces of any terrestrial subject, from which the spirit is separated, and the Spirit itself of that very subject (which is a Spiritual Body) when seven times rectified; and hereby as in a glass you may discern how far that Gross and Earthly Gold I am speaking of, wherewith the Holy City of my brethren is built. In the meanwhile I shall leave with you this Hieroglyphical figure of a star being the mark of this Gold, and also of the city, showing its constituent parts the Water and Fire of the Philadelphians; it manifold and wonderful properties, how it is formed, and how it is made to multiply itself.

www.ingramcontent.com/pod-product-compliance
Lightning Source LLC
LaVergne TN
LVHW041502070426
835507LV00009B/763